This book
was a gift
from

_____

to

_____

A Mother's
Favorite
Lullaby
Book

Running Press
Book Publishers
Philadelphia, Pennsylvania

Printed in Hong Kong.
Canadian representatives: General Publishing Co., Ltd.
30 Lesmill Rd, Don Mills, Ontario M3B 2T6
International representatives: Worldwide Media Services, Inc.
115 East 23rd St., New York, NY 10010

9   8   7   6   5   4   3
The digit on the right indicates the number of this printing.

Library of Congress Card Catalog Number: 84-2060

ISBN: 0-89471-265-9 (library binding)

Cover design by Toby Schmidt.
Illustration by Geri Greinke.
Calligraphy by Judith K. M. Barbour.
Researched and newly edited by T. A. Mossman.
Printed by South Sea International Press.

This book may be ordered by mail from the publisher.
Please include $1.00 postage. But try your bookstore first.
Running Press
Book Publishers
125 South 22nd Street
Philadelphia, Pennsylvania 19103

CONTENTS
(In Alphabetical Order)

Rock-a-Bye, Baby

Rock-a-bye, Baby,
In the tree top.
When the wind blows,
The cradle will rock.
When the bough breaks,
The cradle will fall,
And down will come Baby,
Cradle and all.

Baby is drowsing,
Cozy and fair.
Mother sits near,
In her rocking chair.

Forward and back
The cradle she swings,
And though Baby sleeps,
He hears what she sings.

From the high rooftops
Down to the sea,
No one's as dear
As Baby to me.
Wee little fingers,
Eyes wide and bright~
Now sound asleep
Until morning light.

Baa! Baa! Black Sheep

"Baa! Baa! Black sheep, have you any wool?"
"Yes, kind sir, I've three bags full.
One for my master, and one for my dame,
And one for the little boy
    who lives down the lane."

"Can you weave three blankets for his bed?"
"Yes, to reach from toe to head.
One for his cradle, and one, soft and warm,
And one to keep him tucked in,
    safe from harm."

London Bridge Is Falling Down

London Bridge is falling down,
Falling down,
Falling down.
London Bridge is falling down,
My fair lady.

Baby's cradle's safe and sound,
Safe and sound,
Safe and sound.
Baby's cradle's safe and sound,
My brave laddie.

Guard it 'round with iron bars,

Iron bars,
Iron bars.
Guard it 'round with iron bars,
My fair lady.

Iron bars will rust and bend,
Rust and bend,
Rust and bend.
Iron bars will rust and bend,
My brave laddie.

Guard it, then, with precious gold,
Precious gold,
Precious gold.
Guard it, then, with precious gold,

My fair lady.

Precious gold is fare for thieves,
Fare for thieves,
Fare for thieves.
Precious gold is fare for thieves,
My brave laddie.

Guard it, then, with soldiers strong,
Soldiers strong,
Soldiers strong.
Guard it, then, with soldiers strong,
My fair lady.

Soldiers all are gone to war,

Gone to war,
Gone to war.
Soldiers all are gone to war,
My brave laddie.

Guard it, then, with watchful love,
Watchful love,
Watchful love.
Guard it, then, with watchful love,
My fair lady.

Baby, then, will sleep all night,
Sleep all night,
Sleep all night.
Baby, then, will sleep all night,

My brave laddie.

And she'll grow up straight and tall,
Straight and tall,
Straight and tall.
And she'll grow up straight and tall,
My fair lady.

Lullaby, and Good Night

(Brahms' Lullaby/The Cradle Song)

Lullaby, and good night.
With pink roses bedight,
With lilies o'erspread
Is my baby's sweet head.
Lay you down, now, and rest,
May your slumber be blessed!
Lay you down, now, and rest,
May your slumber be blessed!

Lullaby, and good night.

You're your mother's delight.
Shining angels beside
My darling abide.
Soft and warm is your bed,
Close your eyes and rest your head.
Soft and warm is your bed,
Close your eyes and rest your head.

Sleepyhead, close your eyes.
Mother's right here beside you.
I'll protect you from harm,

You will wake in my arms.
Guardian angels are near,
So sleep on, with no fear.
Guardian angels are near,
So sleep on, with no fear.

Lullaby, and sleep tight.
Hush! My darling is sleeping,
On his sheets white as cream,
With his head full of dreams.
When the sky's bright with dawn,

He will wake in the morning.
When noontide warms the world,
He will frolic in the sun.

My Bonnie Lies Over the Ocean

My bonnie lies over the ocean,
My bonnie lies over the sea,
My bonnie lies over the ocean,
Oh, bring back my bonnie to me!

Chorus:
Bring back, bring back,
Oh, bring back my bonnie to me, to me!
Bring back, bring back,
Oh, bring back my bonnie to me, to me!

Oh, blow ye winds over the ocean,
Oh, blow ye winds over the sea,

Oh, blow ye winds over the ocean,
And bring back my bonnie to me.

Chorus.

Last night when in bed I lay dreaming,
Last night when the moon was on high,
Last night when in bed I lay sleeping,
I thought I heard dear bonnie cry.

Chorus.

My bonnie was sleeping so soundly,
My bonnie was sleeping so tight,
My bonnie was sleeping so soundly,
In his little crib painted white.

Chorus.

The winds, they blew over the ocean,
The winds, they blew over the sea,
The winds, they blew over the ocean,
And brought back my bonnie to me, to me,
And brought back my bonnie to me.

Greensleeves

Alas, my love! You do me wrong
To cast me off discourteously.
For I have lovèd you so long,
Delighting in your company.
Greensleeves was all my joy,
Greensleeves was my delight.
Greensleeves was my heart of gold.
Yea, who but my lady Greensleeves?

I have been ready at your hand,
To grant whatever that you might crave.
I have wagered both life and land,
Your love and good-will for to have.

If you intend thus to disdain,
It doth the more enrapture me.
And even so, I still remain
Your lover in captivity.

My men were clothèd all in green,
And they did ever attend on thee.
All this was gallant to be seen,
And yet thou wouldst not love me.
Thou couldst desire no earthly thing,
But soon thou hadst it readily.
Thy music still I play and sing,
And yet thou wilt not love me.

Well I shall petition God on high,
That thou my constancy mayest see,

And that yet once before I die,
That thou wilt vouchsafe to love me.
Ah, Greensleeves, farewell, adieu,
And God, I trust, shall prosper thee.
For I am still thy lover true.
Come back once more and love me.

Ye watchful guardians of the fair,
Who skim on wings of ambient air,
Of my dear Delia take a care,
And represent her lover
With all the gaiety of youth,
With honor, justice, love, and truth,
Till I return, her passions soothe.
For me in whispers move her.

Be careful no base sordid slave
With soul sunk in a golden grave
Who knows no virtue but to save
With glaring gold bewitch her.
Tell her for me she was designed~
For me, who knows how to be kind,
And have more plenty in my mind
Than one who's ten times richer.

Let all the world turn upside-down,
And fools run an eternal round
In quest of what can ne'er be found,
To please their own ambitions.
Let little minds great charms espy
In shadows which at distance lie,

Whose hoped-for pleasure, when come nigh,
Proves nothing in fruition.

But cast into a mold divine,
Fair Delia does with luster shine.
Her virtuous soul's an ample mine
That yields a constant treasure.
Let poets in sublimest verse
Employ their skills, her fame rehearse,
Let sons of music pass whole days
With well-tuned flutes to please her.

Hush, Little Baby

Hush, little baby, don't say a word,
Daddy's going to buy you a mocking bird.
If that mocking bird don't sing,
Daddy's going to buy you a diamond ring.

If that diamond ring is brass,
Daddy's going to buy you a looking glass.
If that looking glass gets broke,
Daddy's going to buy you a nanny goat.

If that goat don't give no milk,
Daddy's going to buy you a robe of silk.

If that robe of silk gets worn,
Daddy's going to buy you a big French horn.

If that big French horn won't play,
Daddy's going to buy you a candy cane.
If that cane should lose its stripes,
Daddy's going to buy you a set of pipes.

If that set of pipes ain't clean,
Daddy's going to buy you a jumping bean.
If that jumping bean won't roll,
Daddy's going to buy you a lump of coal.

If that lump of coal won't burn,
Daddy's going to buy you a butter churn.

If that butter turns out sour,
Daddy's going to buy you an orchid flower.

If that flower don't smell sweet,
Daddy's going to buy you some salted meat.
If that salted meat won't fry,
Daddy's going to buy you an apple pie.

When that apple pie's all done,
Daddy's going to buy you another one.
When that pie's all eaten up,
Daddy's going to buy you a greyhound pup.

If that dog won't run the course,
Daddy's going to buy you a rocking horse.

If that rocking horse won't rock,
Daddy's going to buy you a cuckoo clock.

And if that cuckoo clock runs down,
You're still the prettiest little boy in town.

Twinkle, Twinkle, Little Star

Twinkle, twinkle, little star,
How I wonder what you are!
Up above the world so high,
Like a diamond in the sky.

Chorus:
Twinkle, twinkle, little star,
How I wonder what you are!

When the blazing sun goes down,
Darkness falls all over town.
Then you show your tiny light,
Twinkling, twinkling through the night.

Chorus.

Weary travelers in the dark
Thank you for your little spark.
Who could see which path to go,
If you did not twinkle so?

Chorus.

In the dark sky you remain,
Peeking through the windowpane,
And you never shut your eye
'Til the sun is in the sky.

Chorus.

As your bright and tiny spark
Lights the traveler in the dark,
Though I know not what you are,
Twinkle, twinkle, little star!

Chorus.

Shenandoah

Oh, Shenandoah, I love your daughter.
Away, you rolling river.
I'll take her 'cross yonder water.

Chorus:
Away, we're bound away.
'Cross the wide Missouri.

Oh, Shenandoah, she took my fancy.
Away, you rolling river.
Oh, Shenandoah, I love your Nancy.

Chorus.

Oh, Shenandoah, I long to see you.

Away, you rolling river.
Oh, Shenandoah, I'm drawing near you.

Chorus.

Oh, Shenandoah, I'm bound to leave you.
Away, you rolling river.
Oh, Shenandoah, I'll ne'er deceive you.

Chorus.

Oh, Shenandoah, I'll ne'er forget you.
Away, you rolling river.
Oh, Shenandoah, I'll ever love you.

Chorus.

Swing Low, Sweet Chariot

<u>Chorus:</u>

Swing low, sweet chariot,
Comin' for to carry me home.
Swing low, sweet chariot,
Comin' for to carry me home.

I looked over Jordan,
And what did I see,
Comin' for to carry me home?
A band of angels comin' after me,
Comin' for to carry me home!

Chorus.

The brightest morning
That ever did dawn ~
Comin' for to carry me home ~
Was the day my baby girl was born.
Comin' for to carry me home.

Chorus.

I'm sometimes up,
And sometimes down.
Comin' for to carry me home.
But still my soul is heavenly-bound.
Comin' for to carry me home.

<u>Chorus.</u>

If you get there
Before I do,
Comin' for to carry me home,
Tell all my friends I'm a-comin' too,
Comin' for to carry me home.

<u>Chorus.</u>

All Through the Night

Sleep, my child, and peace attend thee,
All through the night.
Guardian angels God will send thee,
All through the night.
Soft the drowsy hours are creeping,
Hill and vale in slumber steeping,
Mother here her vigil keeping,
All through the night.

While the moon her watch is keeping,
All through the night;
While the weary world is sleeping,

All through the night;
O'er thy spirit gently stealing,
Visions of delight revealing,
Breathes a pure and holy feeling,
All through the night.

Hark, the whippoorwill is calling,
Clear through the night.
Pure and sweet his notes are falling,
All through the night.
Deep in dreams my baby's lying,
Breezes to my song replying.
Lullabies are softly sighing,
All through the night.

Beautiful Dreamer

Beautiful dreamer, wake unto me.
Starlight and dewdrops are waiting for thee.
Sounds of the rude world, heard in the day,
Lulled by the moonlight, have all passed away.
Beautiful dreamer, queen of my song,
List while I woo thee with sweet melody.
Gone are the cares of life's busy throng.
Beautiful dreamer, awake unto me,
Beautiful dreamer, awake unto me!

Beautiful dreamer, out on the sea
Mermaids are chanting the wild Lorelei.

Over the streamlet vapors are borne,
Waiting to fade at the bright coming morn.
Beautiful dreamer, beam on my heart,
E'en as the morn on the streamlet and sea.
Then will all clouds of sorrow depart.
Beautiful dreamer, awake unto me,
Beautiful dreamer, awake unto me!

Beautiful dreamer, snug in thy bed,
On a silk pillow art resting thy head.
Through the tall willows, night breezes blow,
Wafting sweet songs to young sleepers below.
Beautiful dreamer, love thee I do,
By the same heart that beats strong in my breast.

All the day's troubles and worries are through.
Nothing shall mar thy unsullied rest.
Beautiful dreamer, awake unto me,
Beautiful dreamer, awake unto me!